WIN THE JOB:
Interviewing for Success

John Chisham

Win The Job - Interviewing for Success

Table Of Contents

Win The Job - Interviewing for Success

In this book we will cover:

- The application, resume, and cover letter
- The initial interview (phone)
- The face to face interview
- The questions to ask and to prepare an answer for
- What to do when you leave the interview
- What to do in the days following the interview.

It is my expectation that if you follow this guide, and sprinkle in your personality and your experience that you will come out with a job offer, a raise, or a promotion.

It is my hope that this book helps you attain your career goals.

-John Chisham 3/23

Chapter 1
BEFORE THE INTERVIEW:
THE APPLICATION AND RESUME

Joe had his eye on a job posting he saw online, describing the position he had been desiring all of his life. The company was the tops in the industry he was in. The workplace culture was one that was well-known to be the very best in the industry. The location was minutes from his house. The compensation package included the best health benefits, ownership, and a 401K. The PTO policy was known to be the most generous of any of its kind. This was the opportunity he was looking for, one he could not pass up.

It was also one that others could not pass up. By the time he was able to apply online he was one of over 100 applicants for the job.

Win The Job - Interviewing for Success

Joe knew he needed to set himself apart in some way, so he proceeded to put
together a cover letter and a resume that was sure to impress even the most
discerning hiring authority. By the time he was done, his three page cover letter
and his four page resume was uploaded to the company site.

When the administrator on the company end looked at it, he discarded it after making it through only through half the second page of the cover letter. It was never seen by the one doing the hiring.

"WORKING WITH AN INDUSTRY-SPECIFIC RECRUITER IS THE BEST WAY TO GET A NEW JOB"

Sally went about the process a little differently. She had all the qualifications, but she applied through Indeed. So did one hundred other applicants. Her resume was never seen by anybody but her current boss. Indeed sold her name and her resume to him, unbeknownst to her. She was terminated and now had no job and no prospects.

When it comes down to it, both Sally and Joe made mistakes that an experienced job hunter would never make. Here is the reality: Working with a *good recruiter is the best way to get a new job - and this for several reasons:

- Recruiters know the hidden job market
- Recruiters can help you navigate the process - including resume and cover letter preparation

-Recruiters work directly with the decision makers
 -Recruiters keep your information confidential
- Recruiters negotiate terms on your behalf.

This section may seem a bit self-serving; it is not. I am a specialty construction recruiter, so I only serve in a niche of the literally hundreds of industries out there. Hopefully this book reaches thousands of people and helps them in their job search, and suggesting they use a recruiter will not benefit me directly, unless of course they are in the USA in specialty construction.

I did asterisk the word "good" above. A word of caution; not all recruiters are ethical. Some, like Indeed, will spread your resume out with no regard to your confidentiality.

Others have hidden fees. Still others can ruin the opportunity for you to get the job you are looking for because of the agreements they have with other companies.

So, when looking for a recruiter, here are a few simple tips:

1. Look for a recruiter who specializes in your industry and location
2. Ask for referrals (I frequently give referrals as I am in such a niche industry) for recruiters in your industry.
3. Ask: Do you share my resume or my name with anyone without my permission?
4. Ask: How long will the process take?
5. Ask: Will this cost me anything?
6. Ask: How frequently will you update me?

Win The Job - Interviewing for Success

Although there is no benefit to me in saying this, I am inclined to tell you to work with gpac, the company I work for. They have been in business 32 years, with a sterling reputation. With over 700 recruiters in various markets and industries, there is one who can help you find your next perfect job. If you are interested in learning more, you can send me an e-mail at john.chisham@gogpac.com

Resumes that work

Joe is a real person (not his real name) that I worked with. He is not unique; many people try to stuff all their information into one resume and cover sheet. The resume and cover sheet are a marketing piece that gets you in the door for an interview. When you get the interview, you get to 'fill in the blanks'.

Resumes should **never** exceed two pages. If you have a career like attorney, MD, C-Suite, or professor, you should submit a CV. If you are an engineer or architect, or construction professional, you should add a portfolio of completed projects or a project list. But the resume itself, if possible, should be contained in 1-2 pages. When it comes to resumes, less is more.

Resume writing tips

Resumes should contain the following information:

Win The Job - Interviewing for Success

1. Name
2. Contact information
3. Skills
4. Prior work experience
5. Role description (not generic)
6. Company name with dates of Tenure
7. Education
8. Additional Experience
9. Optional: Awards, achievements, licenses, hobbies, etc.

While there are a few commonly used resume styles, your resume should reflect your unique education, experience and relevant skills. You might consider having multiple versions of your resume tailored to the jobs you're applying for. Here are a few key resume writing tips that will help you organize and design your resume.

1. Look for keywords in the job posting The best place to start when preparing to write a resume is to carefully read the job postings that interest you. You should analyze each job description for common words that show what an ideal candidate looks like for the job. Include those keywords in your resume. If you highlight the skills that employers are looking for, you will have a better chance to get the interview. When you do get the interview, make sure to use those same words in describing your specific skillset.

Win The Job - Interviewing for Success

2. Review resume examples for your industry When you put together your resume, it is a good idea to look at other resumes from similar jobs in your industry. There is a LOT of examples out there just by using 'resume examples for _____" in your search engine. Most writing software (like Word or Pages) feature several styles of resume templates to choose from. It is important to use a style that looks professional and clean.

When you do use a sample, please do not do what Darrin did-copy them word for word. In fact, Darrin actually just substituted his name and contact information without bothering to even change the company names. He got the interview but was quickly exposed as a fraud. He was blackballed in the industry afterwards. Use the templates as a guide but put your own experiences etc. in them.

3. Make it simple and easy to read. Most resume samples are one page, and they keep them very simple. This is because it is a simple introduction of you, your background, and your specific skills that are relevant. I review hundreds of resumes every month. The ones that make me dig, I immediately reject. Employers do not have time to digest a resume that is too heavy on information.

4. More is NOT better Including only the most relevant information and skills means employers can consume more information about you, and more quickly understand your qualifications for the role, making it more likely you will get the interview. Your experience as a burger flipper is only relevant at fast food restaurants, not that high powered marketing job you are currently looking at applying for.

STAND OUT FROM THE CROWD

Anatomy of a Perfect Resume

1 **JOSÉ SMITH** **2** 518 Woodfield Rd, Chicago, IL 60652
555-212-8533 • jose_smith807@gmail.com

3 KEY SKILLS

Soft Skills
Brand Positioning & Storytelling
Project Management
Team Leadership
Communication

Hard Skills
Google Analytics
Marketo
Salesforce
Excel

4 PRIOR WORK EXPERIENCE

Umbrella Corp.
Dec. 2016 - Present
Marketing Intern

- Collaborated with a team of 4 people to brainstorm 3 major creative campaigns which ultimately drove 100,000+ web site visits and a 27% year-over-year increase in traffic
- Drafted copy for 3 ebooks and associated email marketing campaigns, resulting in 10,000 downloads and 3,000 new leads generated
- Analyzed data from Google Analytics and Marketo to optimize marketing efforts moving forward, leading to a 24% increase in downloads from campaign 2 to campaign 3

5

6 Coffee 2 Go
Sep. 2012 - Dec. 2016
Barista, Shift Manager

- Served 50-100 customers per day, driving roughly $800 per day in sales
- Consistently upsold offerings and daily specials, resulting in an average yearly revenue increase of 12%
- Trained, managed, and coordinated schedules for a team of 6 in order to ensure top-quality customer service

7 EDUCATION

Springfield University Sep. 2012 - Dec. 2016
Bachelors of Business Administration (Specialization in Marketing)
Graduated Summa Cum Laude with a 3.7 GPA

8 ADDITIONAL EXPERIENCE

- Recipient of the Springfield University Hispanic Marketing Society's Rising Star Award, *April 2016*
- Volunteer, Springfield Animal Rescue
- Avid cyclist and jazz piano player

9

glassdoor

5. Include provable numbers. Hiring authorities LOVE metrics. There are two reasons that you will get hired: you will SAVE or MAKE the company money. Using numbers that highlight these types of values always get the attention of hiring authorities. An example might be:

"Incorporated processes that saved the company 15% year over year" or " Increased profitability of my project by 25%

6. Use a professional font As stated, employers are busy people. Do not make them work to read your resume. Use a standard font like Arial or Times New Roman or Georgia. Make the font 10-12 points Because employers have only a short time to review your resume, it should be as clear and as easy to read as possible.

7. Include only relevant information and put it first You get six seconds for your resume (on average) to be read. So, put the most relevant experience up top, using an economy of words (preferably keywords). Try to include only work experience, achievements, education and skills most relevant to the employer.

8. Use active language Your resume should be filled with action words that communicate in the most concise manner. This saves space but also makes it more interesting. Use words like "spearheaded" "achieved," "earned," "led" or "accomplished." Also, and this is common sense, have a couple of trusted friends or colleagues read it and let you know if it seems long, muddled, or boring.

9. Call attention to important achievements As stated earlier, pointing to specific achievements supported by numbers and described with action words is a great way to get your resume noticed. Better than just writing out your duties is to highlight **keyword** skills and what you have done in regards to them.

10. Proofread and edit Make sure that you comb your resume for errors. Better yet, have a trusted friend or colleague proofread and edit it. And, if you know a business owner in a related industry, you might have them review it as well.

11. Decide whether you need a unique resume for different jobs Sometimes, people craft several resumes to highlight different skill sets. You need to decide if it is important for you to do the same. In marketing, we sometimes do what is called a split test; the same can be done with a resume. Experiment with different formats and fonts to see which one gets the best response.

Finally,it is important to remember a resume never got anyone a job; it is the interview that does it. But a resume is the way you get your foot in the door! So pay close attention to the suggestions I have given and you will increase your chances of getting the interview, and the job.

How to deliver the resume

Win The Job - Interviewing for Success

If you are using (as recommended) a recruiter, they will hand deliver your resume to the hiring authority. If they are good, they will expand on your background to get you the interview. But what if you decide (not recommended) to try to get a job on your own? Here are some tips on getting your resume to the right spot.

1. Follow instructions on website: It is not a good thing to ever apply online; you just are one of hundreds. But if that is the only way, follow the instructions to a T.

2. If you can, hand deliver the resume to the place of employment. Better yet, find the hiring manager and hand it to them while introducing yourself.

3. Never, and I mean never, post your resume on recruiting websites like Indeed, Glassdoor, or Zip Recruiter: As stated earlier these are marketing companies, and they use your resume to market you - and there is a good chance your employer will see it or hear of it from colleagues in the industry. If you are employed and MUST post your resume on one of those sites to apply, be careful to mark it private. If you have no job currently, you should mark it private so that you do not get calls from companies who have nothing to do with your desired job.

4. Follow up Once submitting your application and resume, make sure to follow up with a phone call within 48 hours. Continue following up until you get a definitive answer

2.
Before the Interview: Targeting your next employer

I was going to be a professional Baseball player.

I mean, I grew up in San Diego. I always wanted to play for the Padres. I believed I could play shortstop for the Padres. Through the age of 12 , I still had a chance, I mean, I was long and lanky, had some athleticism, and I played little league.

A stint in college and state amateur teams quickly brought me to reality. Facing pitchers in NCAA Division 2 that could throw 90 MPH and a breaking ball that looked like the shape of a banana and drop 3 feet was only part of it. My speed and agility notwithstanding, the lack of ability to do anything but get base hits against these pitchers made me realize that my dreams would never be my reality.

However, it took a long time of languishing and wasting time in these amateur leagues (it was fun, though) before I really got the message.

The funny and sad thing is when I left my last amateur team, there was a couple of 40 year olds that still didn't get the message that the big leagues were not going to be calling soon.

Years later, when I was an umpire for amateur baseball, there were still those guys. I mean today, when I golf, there are people I play with that believe that they will make the PGA tour someday. I always believed that I could make the Champions Tour when I turned 50. But my lowest handicap index to date is a 7.6- and that is based on a course that is under 6800 yards.

Watching how the short hitters on the Champions Tour hit it 60 yards beyond my distance and in the middle the fairway does enough to trounce my dreams before I see how their short game is and it demolishes any hopes.

The moral of the story is that we all have dreams, and we ought to pursue them. In this world of participation trophies, we are led to believe that we ought to be able to win at anything we try. When it comes to your job search, you need to be realistic - or else you need to learn to live with disappointment. You do not get the job you want because you tried. You must bring something of value to the table and actually be qualified to do the job.

So this is where we start.

Your job search needs to start with reality.

Win The Job - Interviewing for Success

As a recruiter, this is where I begin. I look at your resume, specifically at recent experience. I ask you questions related to that experience. I then dig in on 5 other areas:

1. Location
2. Compensation
3. Culture
4. Career Trajectory/Growth
5. Title/Position

So to effectively target your your next employer you need to do the search based upon these criteria.

Win The Job - Interviewing for Success

1. Location So many people that I talk to regret neglecting this one question in their job search. Prior to COVID, commuting to an office was something most people did. I speak to some people whose commute is sometime over 2 hours one way! That is four hours of daily life you never get back. Additionally, with gasoline being over $6.00 a gallon in some parts of the country this becomes part of the consideration.

So where do you want to work?

Do you want to drive to an office? Do you want to work from home? Do you want a hybrid role?

This is the most basic consideration when targeting your job search is the location as well as the stance of the company on hybrid or work from home.

My most basic searches start here. You can do a search on Google for all the companies that do what you do within the area you are looking. Here is my search for drywall contractors in Sioux Falls, SD.

After doing the search, you can very easily look on each website to see if there is any jobs posted, and if you are a fit for the job. Of course, you can use the online application form and submit a resume. Make sure to take note of the name of the owner of the company and any contact information you can get from the site.

Win The Job - Interviewing for Success

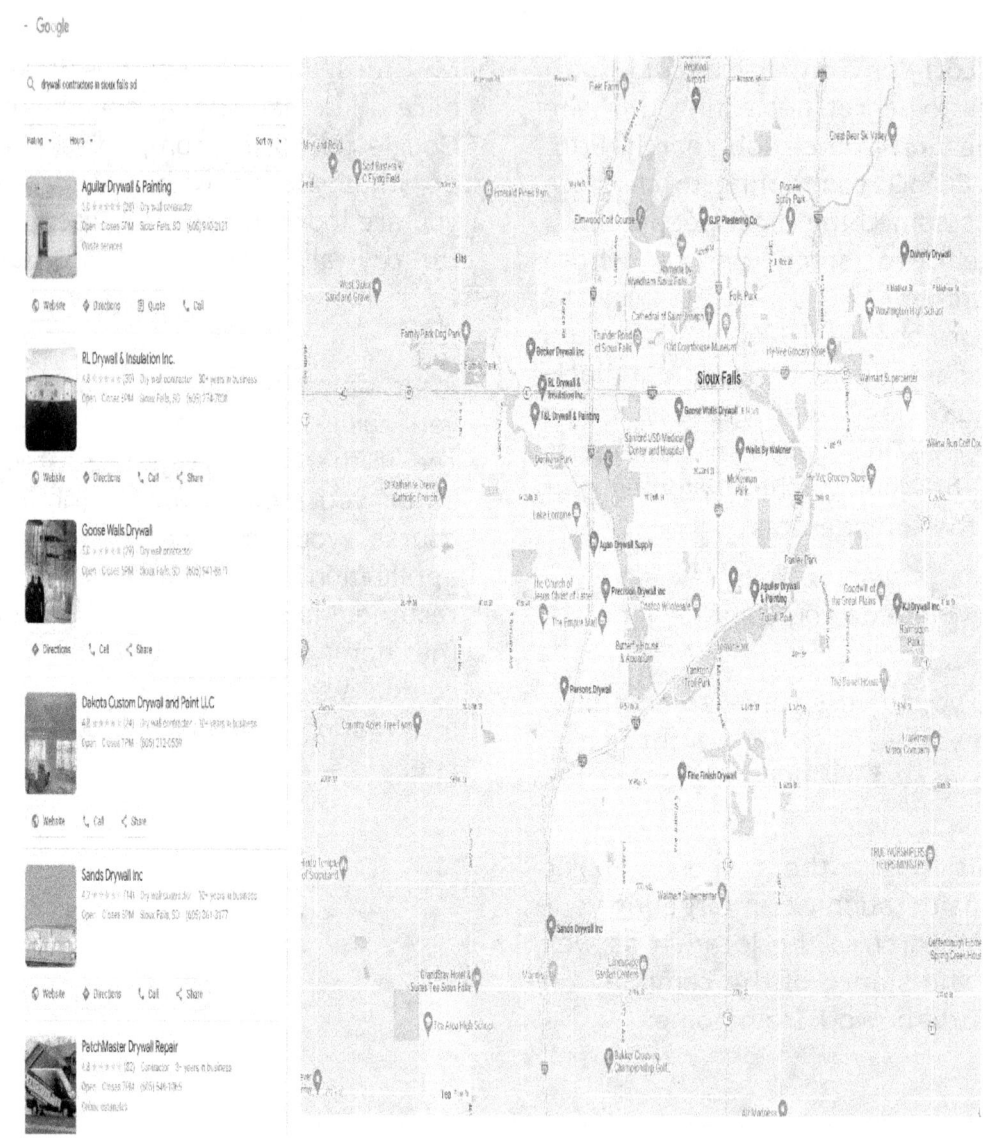

Win The Job - Interviewing for Success

The next step I take is a quick search on Indeed and other posting sites to see what is out there in terms of advertised jobs. The cool thing here is that you can set up an alert for whenever a new job is posted so you get a notification. The Indeed job board is like others, some will list a salary, and a job description. Make sure to take note of the job description and modify your resume as needed with key words and relevant skills.

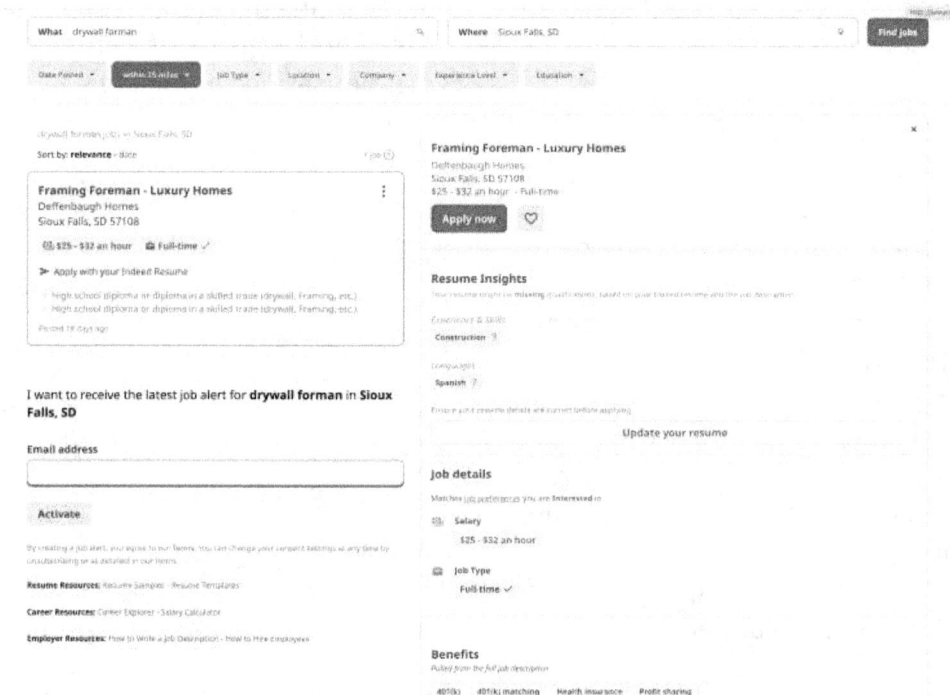

Here is a pro tip: You can put the name of your company in the Indeed search box and be informed whenever they post a job online. This will give you the chance in the future to apply for that next job on the ladder through internal means!

2. Compensation Location is important, but so also is compensation. When you are hunting for a job, you need to make sure that you understand that a job is more than just an hourly wage or an annual salary. You need to make a list of what is important to you in terms of compensation:

- Hourly salary, wage, or commission- what is your minimum you ned?
-Needed benefits- medical, dental, vision, life, disability
- Retirement- ESOP company? 401K? Profit sharing?
- Bonuses
-Car allowance?
Mileage compensation? Gas card?
- Other benefits (cell phone, I pad, laptop)
- Group discounts (gym, health, mobile phone plan, etc.)

Make sure you do a budget and figure out the minimum salary that you can make work. Start there and move up. Remember, if that minimum includes money you need to spend for health insurance, you can subtract that amount if health is provided. Same thing for you budget for a car and gas if there is compensation for mileage.

Win The Job - Interviewing for Success

It is important to consider what the wage is. I can tell you this (we will cover it in the interview chapters) that the most important thing is advertised salaries are a range based on experience. It is in the interview where you build value for what you bring to the company, those budgeted numbers can go out the window. If you make the company believe they need you based on the value you bring, the more you will get paid. Conversely, if you undervalue yourself and what you bring, there is a good chance you will get paid below what you are really worth until you can prove yourself.

That is the bottom line.

Trusting the interview methods and the verbiage I will teach you in these later chapters will get you paid what you are worth.

"IF YOU MAKE THE COMPANY BELIEVE THEY NEED YOU BASED ON THE VALUE YOU BRING, THE MORE YOU WILL GET PAID."

3. Culture - Culture is a popular byword when it comes to the modern working world. Don't get me wrong- culture is extremely important. But, what is culture? The following is a working definition:

Company culture is the synthesis of values, vision, mission, and purpose that sits at the center of any successful business. It is the cohesive atmosphere that permeates a company and directly affects the way people work within that company. Culture to a company is like mindset in an individual. It is what sets a company apart from others and determines the overall performance of the company.

Many companies try to create 'culture' but it is not something that can be fabricated by hip furniture, open working areas, company perks etc. Those can be the visual or manifestations of a good culture, but it is not culture. Let's break down the working definition and how you can determine from the outside looking in what the culture is.

Values, Vision, Mission, and Purpose - This is the 'why' of the company. It involves both the 'what' we do and 'how' we do it. A good company

A good company culture will always align what they do with how they do it and why they do it. Without the 'why' there is no culture. When any of these parts get disconnected, there is a palpable change in culture.

Win The Job - Interviewing for Success

How do you discover this from the outside? Look at the website and observe if the company has a statement about their values, vision, mission and purpose. If those align with how you do work, and are able to get an interview, you should ask questions of those interviewing you how those statements align with how the company actually does business. (Some detailed questions will be shared in Chapter 5 of this book.)

Cohesive atmosphere This is the how the people in the company interact with one another, performance expectations, and how they work. Is this a 'family' atmosphere where we have connection outside of work? It is a 'work hard/play hard" atmosphere where the company is high pressure to produce but when work is done or goals are completed we can get out and 'play' during the work day at the office? Does the company have an aggressive or passive way they work with customers? Do people collaborate on projects or are they judged and compensated purely on what they bring to the table? Is there expectations that you will be at your desk from 9-5, or is there a more flexible work schedule?

What sets the company apart This is really hard to put a finger on looking from the outside. This is the alignment of the vision and values with how the company delivers its' product. In some situations, it is the product that sets the company apart, in other cases, it is the people and how they deliver the product which sets it apart.

Starting with the website is a good place to go. Also, company reviews on sites like Google or product review sites. People will often reflect on not only the product but the customer service. The Better Business Bureau is another good site to look at to understand how the company handles complaints. You need to take it with a grain of salt; a lot of times there are people who can never be satisfied. Balance the good with the bad.

Finally, asking good questions during the interview is key. I will cover culture questions in Chapter 5.

This is difficult to discover from the outside, but you can ascertain some information through looking at the website, social media posts, and company reviews on sites like Glassdoor. Beware of the Glassdoor reviews- like any other online reviews, you need to balance the obvious disgruntled former employees' opinion with those who are currently working there. I place a lot more credence on the long term employee reviews.

4. Career Trajectory/Growth

Another reason people look for a new job is that they have been stuck in the same position for a number of years. In my niche, a good example is an assistant project manager that is desirous of becoming a project manager.

When doing a targeted job search, look for those specific titles, and determine if you have even the most basic requirements to take the leap into that next step. Trust me, if it is determined that you do a hiring authority will jump at the chance to train someone into that role that may be at the company long term.

When looking at your next job, it is also important to ascertain whether there is a clear path to continued growth. Sometimes, this will be right in the job posting. This is also something that you can search out on the website in the 'About Us' or similar section. Oftentimes, this section will highlight the career paths of long-tenured employees.

This is the best evidence of career trajectory and growth. Once again, this is a part of the interview strategies I will be discussing in chapter ___ about great questions to ask during the interview.

5. Title/position

This is self explanatory. You need to target your job search according to the next title or position you are seeking - or willing and able to do. As stated in the last section, you may not be qualified at your current company to hold that position, but another company may see your experience and be willing to train you and give you that position now instead of having to wait.

I opened this chapter with an illustration about my dreams of being a baseball player. A lot of job seekers I deal with are unrealistic in their job search. A project manager for an IT company, for example, is not a project manager for a construction company. The skill sets simply do not transfer. Similarly, there are major differences between working for a construction contractor and sub contractor. The sub- contractor is focussed on a specific aspect of construction- a specialist. I run into this one frequently, where a sub- contractor specialist wants to work for a general contractor, and expects to get paid the same. This is simply not realistic, as you must be trained in all the other scopes of con. If you choose to change careers midstream, or do not have the requisite knowledge to do the job, or you must prove it, you will take a pay cut.

Win The Job - Interviewing for Success

But that is okay - there are certainly times in your life that you need a change and temporary setbacks in position or compensation are fine. If this is one of those times you should go for it. The market has its ups and downs and there are opportunities that come about as a result of that. However, if you find yourself caught in a down market, your best value may be in your current role based on your current skills, talents and abilities.

"IF YOU CHOOSE TO CHANGE CAREERS MIDSTREAM, OR DO NOT HAVE THE REQUISITE KNOWLEDGE TO DO THE JOB, OR YOU MUST PROVE IT, YOU WILL TAKE A PAY CUT"

7 tips for a successful job hunt

I understand, believe me.

Looking for a new job can be a challenging process and can be overwhelming. The key to being successful is a proper mindset and managing yourself and your emotions and attitude. Your mindset and attitude will determine if your job search is a success or failure.

Remember, your new job is out there, and you can find it. By refining your mindset and having a positive attitude, you can become an effective and successful job seeker- and that translates into becoming a great employee!

Here are my top tips to help you avoid feeling overwhelmed:

Win The Job - Interviewing for Success

1. NOT JUST ANY JOB, BUT THE JOB Know what you want, but be realistic. I get so many applications from people who appear to never read the job posting I put out! It is so important that you know what you are looking for. Do you have the skills, talents, and abilities to do the job?Do you want the job? Be focussed and be realistic.

2. DON'T GENERALIZE If you use one standard resume or CV for every job application, you're missing an opportunity to really sell yourself. Keep the same framework, but also read the job posting and use it to skill match, keyword optimize and showcase your relevant achievements and experience.

3. SET A SCHEDULE Getting a job is your job. Set a daily schedule, just like you are working. Set goals for yourself. Maintain a spread sheet of where you have applied and interviewed. Use it to regularly follow up on your applications and interviews.

4. MANAGE YOUR PERSONAL BRAND As well as owning a great resume and/or CV, maintaining a professional and engaging social media presence - and most importantly a great LinkedIn profile - is critical to your career success.

5. USE YOUR NETWORK Networking is a needed skill when it comes to seeking a job. About 80 percent of all jobs are filled through personal and professional connections. Again, this has made using platforms like LinkedIn even more beneficial. You can network with owners and hiring managers you never would have known. Be very active in reaching out and connecting to a great network of people who do what you do.

6. STAY POSITIVE To get the right job, you may need to send multiple resumes, fill out many applications, and sit through many interviews. Rejection at any stage can wear you down. Learn what you can from every part of the process, and realize that every no is getting you closer to a yes. Stay positive and keep your mindset strong

7. USE A RECRUITER At the end of the day, the very best person you can talk to is an industry-specific recruiter. A good recruiter knows how to market- and will use your resume and information they get from you and make sure that every appropriate employer in the area knows about your background and experience. The good ones have direct connections with the decision makers in those businesses and are aware of the hidden job market - those jobs that are not advertised. Finally, they are your best resource for reviewing resumes and interview preparation, as well as negotiating the best offer on your behalf.

Chapter 3:
BEFORE THE INTERVIEW:
PREPARING FOR THE INTERVIEW

An interview is first and foremost a business meeting.

Specifically, it is a sales meeting.

You are selling yourself, and the company is selling itself.

You got the interview with a marketing piece, your resume and your cover letter.

If you used a good recruiter, they prepared a marketing piece to present you to a variety of different companies that fit the bill.

Now, the proof is in the pudding. How the interview goes is largely up to you.

Win The Job - Interviewing for Success

No need to be nervous. There are several things you can do to be ready for an in-person interview.

THE DAY BEFORE

Get your car washed

This is an important step. You will be amazed at the things people look at. You do not want your vehicle to look lived in. So, the day before your interview, make sure your interior is clean and neat- no obvious garbage laying about.

Get the exterior washed and looking good as well. Even a beater can look good if it is cleaned and kept neat.

Google your route

You want to make sure you know how to get there, and how long it will take. Pro Tip: Do the search around the same time you will be departing your home or office for the interview to get a good idea of the affect traffic will have on your drive. Build an extra 15 minute cushion in so you can be at the interview 10 minutes early.

Review the website (and other info)

You should have already done this in preparing your resume and cover letter, but a quick review will be helpful in preparing yourself.

Win The Job - Interviewing for Success

Having knowledge about the company, how long it has been around, the type of work they do, and some knowledge about the person interviewing you will be helpful. It also will impress the people who are interviewing you that you know about the company. It will also help you with 'power phrase 1" which will be discussed in the next chapter.

Practice responses to questions you will be asked

Chapter 5 has an exhaustive list of questions you can ask, and how to answer some common interviewer questions. Here are a few of the most common:

- What kind of job are you looking for?
- Why are you looking to move on from your current company?

- What are your strengths?
- Your weaknesses?
- What do you know about our Company?
- Why did you choose your particular vocation?
- What are your qualifications?

In preparing to answer the questions, here are a few hints:

- Don't lie. Always answer questions **truthfully** and as "to the point" as possible.
- Don't ever make **derogatory** remarks about your present or former employers or companies.
- Don't **"over answer"** questions. - The interviewer may steer the conversation in to politics or economics. Be **honest**, but not opinionated (unless the job calls for it). **Say as little as possible.**

Win The Job - Interviewing for Success

A little more on the "over" answering questions. There are really two types of questions you will be asked. "What time Is it?" These are questions that can answered directly.

Example:

Q. "how many years of experience do you have for this role"

A. "I have 10 years project management experience"

"How do you build a clock?" These questions take a bit more explanation. You do not want to over answer, but you also want to give enough information.

Example: Q. "Tell us how you run your projects"

A. "I start by doing A, I continue on to B, then C, finally I do D and if needed follow up with an E." Then ask *"Is that enough information? Would you like me to provide more?*

Remember, be honest, be direct, and to the point. If you are not sure if you have provided enough information, ask.

Prepare a list of questions you will ask/need answered

These can be written down in a portfolio/binder. Here are some basic questions: (more questions in chapter 5
- A detailed description of the position?

Win The Job - Interviewing for Success

- Reason the position is available?
-Anticipated indoctrination and training program
-Advanced training programs available for those who demonstrate outstanding ability?
-Earnings of those successful people in their third to fifth year?
- Company growth plans?
- The next step?

If the questions are answered in the normal course of the interview, you can cross them out in the notepad so you do not repeat the question. Be prepared to take notes and write down the answers to the questions so you can review it later.

One question you must never ask is the money question. When you ask that question it makes it look like you are not interested in what you bring to the table, only what you will get paid. This goes for **compensation, vacation, bonus, retirement, and benefits.**

That being said, you do need to prepare on how to answer the money question. It all starts with your introduction, and you need to prepare the following statement in your own words:

"Mr/Ms/Mrs.____ Thanks for this opportunity to interview with your company. I have done some research, and I am excited to learn more about your company and about where it has been and where it is going"

The above statement is used in different forms throughout the interview- at the beginning, middle, and end. I will explain further in the next chapter; however you do need to use it if and when the money question is asked.

Win The Job - Interviewing for Success

Q. How much money do you need?

A. Mr/Ms/Mrs ____, As I said earlier, I am very excited to learn about the company and the role I would be playing if hired. I have not been disappointed! So let us suffice it to say, I am very interested in the opportunity, and I believe if you think I am a good fit, you will make me a fair offer based upon my skills and talents I bring to the table. And I would be excited to look at any fair offer."

If they press the issue, and you are currently in a job, you can answer " I am accustomed to making X with Y benefits. You do not have to answer this question in some states, but an honest and direct answer is better.

More on this in the 5th chapter.

Pick out what you will wear

Make sure it is appropriate for the type of job you are applying for. A tuxedo is not appropriate to wear for an interview to be a janitor. However, you should still at the least be dressed 'business casual'. This looks differently in different areas of the world. What is important is that it is clean, pressed, and without holes, rips, or stains.

Win The Job - Interviewing for Success

Wear what feels comfortable, but not too comfortable. If you are old school and want to wear a tie and a coat, or a real nice dress, go for it. Some people say dress for the job you want next- others say do not look better than the people who are going to be interviewing you. The key is comfort and confidence. This does not mean being too casual, however. Under no circumstances should you go to an interview in 'casual' clothes like sweat pants, shorts, a tee shirt, or yoga pants - unless of course part of your interview process is a workout.

Get a good nights sleep

There is truth to the advertising campaign that encourages you to stay at a certain hotel chain prior to a business meeting. This is because it is important to get a good nights sleep, especially when you are going to be interviewing. Like any other

business context, interviewing requires quick thought and attention to the task. You will feel most confident in yourself and up to the task at hand if you are well rested.

THE DAY OF THE INTERVIEW

Hopefully, you are well rested and ready to go and confident in your presentation.

You got yourself dressed, ate a good breakfast, and you are getting into your clean vehicle, and you have your route prepared. You are planning on getting to the interview site 15 minutes prior to the interview. There are several steps on the day of the interview prior to the interview you should consider.

Appearance:

Win The Job - Interviewing for Success

You have already picked out your interview outfit. When combing your hair, if you are wearing a jacket, comb your hair with the jacket off. Make sure your nails are trimmed and neat. Limit your jewelry- nothing religious or political- (unless appropriate for the job you are applying for). Be conservative and middle of the road. Dress for success- not for offense. Remember, this is all part of how the company will see you representing them.

Smell good - but not too good.

It should go without saying that you should bathe prior to the interview, so I wont go into that. It is important to remember when applying cologne or perfume to be very conservative.

The scent you apply should not be overpowering. The best bet is to avoid it all together as you are not going on a date, you are going on an interview.

Pay attention to your breath. Make sure you brush your teeth and use mouthwash. If you are going to drink coffee or tea, make sure you use a mint or breath spray prior to the interview.

A word to smokers and smokeless tobacco users: If you must smoke, remember the smell of smoke lingers and sticks. This could be offensive to people. Make sure your breath and your clothes so not smell like a smokestack. If you chew tobacco, check your teeth before going into the interview. Refrain from chewing anything during the interview- including gum.

What to bring in to the interview

Win The Job - Interviewing for Success

- **Resume** Make sure that you have a copy of your resume, and review it thoroughly to be prepared to discuss all the points

- **Work Samples** that are relevant to the job; nothing proprietary. A construction project manager might bring examples of building projects he or she has completed.

- **A folder, a pen, and a notepad.** I recommend using a portfolio to keep the resume neat and the notes at hand. You should have questions written down, and having a notepad allows you to take notes during the interview to review later. It also is helpful when there are multiple people to jot down their names for future reference.

- **Phone numbers and address** of the interview site in case you are running late, accident, etc.

- **References** Bring names and phone numbers of people you have worked with and for. Of course, you want to make sure they are aware that they are a reference and that they will paint a positive picture of your work.

- **Anything they ask you to bring.**

What to leave in the car

- **Mobile phones** are a great tool, but they are also a huge distraction. When going into the interview the best bet is to leave the phone in the car.

- **Smart watch** I would leave it in the car as well or turn notifications off. The worst thing you can do in an interview is look at your watch or phone. It demonstrates a lack of interest on your part.

Win The Job - Interviewing for Success

- Gum, chewing tobacco, cigarettes
- Weapons

Many people do not think of the wait as an important part of the interview- but it is. Walk in, introduce yourself confidently to the receptionist, and take a seat. You can review your notes, write down any questions you may have thought of when walking in, and review your answers again. You can also practice mindfulness and get calm before the interview.

You may be asked to fill out an application. If this is the case, fill it out fully, neatly, and truthfully. Do not leave blanks or refer to your resume.

The important thing is to remember you are there to complete a task. Having your head down in your phone or occupied in playing a game or texting is a bad look to employers. They see what you do while you wait as a reflection of how you will represent their company.

At the end of the day, being prepared is a crucial task in getting the job. Remember, this is a business meeting. You are there to sell yourself to the company. Coming in prepared and confident will go a long way in determining not only if you get the job, but how much you are compensated up front. Taking heed of these tips will give you an excellent chance of success - meaning getting a job offer.

Chapter 4.
REASONS FOR REJECTION:
AVOIDING THE PITFALLS

A major reason people fail in the interview process is the same reason they fail in just about any other area of life.

Lack of preparation.

Thats why you have bought this book!

In chapter 2, we looked at targeting your next employer. It is my hope that my story on desiring to play baseball professionally helped you understand that there are things we want to do and desire to do, but simply do not have the hard skills to do.

Win The Job - Interviewing for Success

In chapter 3, we looked at preparing for the interview from getting your car washed to getting dressed for success all the way to preparing a route that will get you into the place 15 minutes early.

In chapter 5, we will look at questions you need to be ready to answer, as well as questions you should be prepared to ask.

It is all about preparation.

Hopefully, you have taken the time to research and target those places that match location, skill set, compensation, and culture. You have prepared by knowing as much as you can about the company based on their website, their Glassdoor site, people who have worked there, etc.

There are multiple major reasons for rejection, reasons why you might not get the job. I feel before we go into the actual interview process, we need to address these reasons for rejection because you must prepare for these as well. In being aware of reasons that employers reject potential employees we can avoid the pitfalls and make our job search more successful- and efficient.

REASONS FOR REJECTION

There are probably more reasons for rejection, but I want to address some of the major ones I have heard in debriefing the interview with hundreds of hiring authorities over the years.

Attitude

Win The Job - Interviewing for Success

One of the top reasons for rejection has to do with poor attitudes. For example, in an effort to impress, many candidates come across as arrogant. There is a fine line between confidence in your abilities and arrogance. Confidence is data based; you have the numbers to prove that you can do what you say you can do. In the construction industry, for example, we commonly have a portfolio of completed jobs (or project list) that breaks down the role you played, the scopes you personally supervised, and the success(es) of the job (profit, ahead of schedule, under budget, etc). A proven track record and an acknowledgement of other peoples' contributions makes it look less like bragging and arrogance.

Another attitude to keep an eye on is a **'know it all' attitude.** The worst thing you can do is come into a job interview - or a job- believing you know everything there is to know. We all are continually learning and improving. There is nobody who is all -knowing. If you are not growing in a career, you are dying. Potential employers love to hear things like "I have learned to do it this way- but I would love to learn from you how you approach it".

A close cousin to the know it all is the **"this is the right way" or 'this is the way I have always done it"** These types of statements come off as arrogant, and they also close off conversation and show you are unwilling to change and grow. Be careful not to make absolute statements

It is better to say something to the effect of 'this is the way I have always done it, but I would not be here if I wasn't willing to learn a better way". Always answer questions in such a way to keep the discussion going.

Along with arrogance, there can be too much **humility.** Being conditioned not to brag, or fearing coming across as arrogant, some candidates are reluctant to describe their accomplishments. Again, there is a fine line between humility and being truly humble. Being truly humble is very attractive. It is being open to learning. It is acknowledging when you do something well, but understanding we all can improve. It is never being satisfied with just 'good enough' or with yesterday's accomplishments. Successful interviews include expressing what you can bring to a company while acknowledging success is a team sport.

Appearance

I have coached people preparing for interviews for years, and I am convinced that many candidates do not consider their appearance as much as they should. I once had a person show up in a v-neck shirt and sweat pants to a mid-level management interview that I told him would be business casual. I had a young lady show up in yoga pants and a half shirt for an estimating interview. The hiring authority commented that she was appropriately dressed if she was interviewing to do a spinning class.

First impressions are made in the first three to five minutes. Whether you like it or not, people do judge a book by its cover. In chapter 3 we covered some basics of appearance.

Win The Job - Interviewing for Success

You must be clean and neat, with combed hair. and fresh breath. Clothing should be worn that is appropriate to the position which you are applying for. Dress for success- not offense. If you have a question about how to dress, it is not wrong to ask someone. If you are working with a recruiter, ask them. If you are not, call the person you are interviewing with and ask them. The best rule of thumb is to dress for the position above the one you are interviewing for - and never show up in anything short of basic business casual.

Social Media Profiles

It amazes me to this day how people do not realize that your social media profiles are there for everyone to see. One of the top reasons people still get rejected for a job is that their social media profile kills them. It is just like appearance; your social media profile makes a statement that declares to the world who you want them to believe you are. And, if that includes smoking pot (even where it is legal), doing keg stands, or your spring break pictures you are not likely to get hired.

I cannot tell you how many times a person I work with has crushed the interview, only not to receive an offer because of their social media profile. And, just like political office, this stuff does not disappear. A job offer was once rescinded for a client of mine who had a picture of a marijuana leaf on a Facebook page from 5 years prior.

Win The Job - Interviewing for Success

The most important presentation is on your LinkedIn website where you can build a great resume. Make sure that site is kept insulated from political, religious, or other things that distract from your professional profile. Facebook, Instagram, Twitter, etc. are all more for fun and social- but if your grandma or grandpa shouldn't see it, neither should a potential employer.

This is not the time to scream first amendment issues. Make your social media private at the very least if it does not paint a favorable picture of you. If you are not sure, have someone from an older generation like your parents or grandparents give you an honest opinion.

It is painfully obvious when candidates haven't learned about the job, company or industry prior to the interview. As we covered in chapter 2, it is vital that you take the time to do some basic background on the company you are interviewing with prior to applying. When you secure the interview, it is a great time to take that research to the next level.

Lack of research

Win The Job - Interviewing for Success

Using the Internet to research the company is probably the most common way today to do it. Start with their website. This will give you a good feel for the company - but that is only what they want their customers to know. Remember, the website is a marketing piece. You need to dig deeper into what makes them tick. Check out Google, go to the trade association they are a part of. In the construction industry, we have the blue book for construction as an example. There is also sites like Glassdoor. As mentioned in Chapter 2, you need to read those ratings with a grain of salt. Balance the experience of former employees with the current ones. Also, note the tenure of the employees on their profiles.

Just like they will do with you, a good way to find out about a company is to look them up on social media.

On their social media sites, you can connect with people who work at the company you are applying to.

My favorite place to start is LinkedIn. On LinkedIn, you can look up the company and it will provide a list of people that work there. You can reach out to them, offer to connect, and ask some questions about the company. Of course, you can go offline as well. You can talk with friends, peers and other professionals about what they know of the company you are interviewing with.

Not relating skills to employers' needs.

Sort of like showing up to interview for a janitorial position in a tuxedo, listing sterling accomplishments means little if you can't relate them to a company's requirements.

Win The Job - Interviewing for Success

I see a lot of resumes that list the accomplishment of the 18 year old you becoming an Eagle Scout. While that is a great accomplishment, and something to be very proud of, if you cannot relate it to the job you are applying for, it does do much good for you to bring it up. In order to make it relevant, you might pull some experiences you had or skills you learned while accomplishing that achievement.

This all goes back to the preparation of your resume. Discover the sills needed for the particular job for which you are applying. Then, as you prepare your resume, and your interview, use past experiences whether at work, or in athletics, or clubs or volunteer opportunities to highlight your unique set of skills that relate to the job you are applying for.

Reiterate your skills and convince the employer that you can "do the same for them." Having done research on the company and what they do will be to your advantage. As you will have some understanding about the skills you need to relate.

Handling salary issues ineptly.

The very worst thing you can do is go into a job interview thinking all about compensation. While it is an important issue, it cannot be communicated as the most important issue. Employers rightly believe that most people who talk too much about compensation will leave that job for the first bump in pay that comes along. So the way we communicate about salary is very important- so important in fact, I dedicate significant space on it in chapter 3 and chapter 5. Pay good attention to the verbiage I use because - well- it works.

Win The Job - Interviewing for Success

Candidates often ask about salary and benefit packages too early in the conversation. So rule number one is not to bring compensation up. It is better to pay attention to all the other aspects of the job first and foremost.

I don't know about you, but there are things I would NEVER do no matter the money. So, if I do not like the manager, or the job description, or the culture, I probably am not going to work there anyway. Better to discover if you want to work there first before diving into money. Also, it is important to build value in what you bring to the table before talking about money. That conversation becomes easier if you prove to the person interviewing you that you are a person they must have.

The other mistake that candidates make in terms of compensation is putting numbers out there.

If they believe an employer is interested, and have an inflated value of the skills they bring, they name a very high number- and price themselves out of the jobs. Conversely, they may be ill-informed about the value of a person in their position, and ask for too little. In that way you undervalue yourself or appear desperate. This is why I encourage you to allow the interviewer to bring up compensation and in your answer do not name a number but instead indicate you will look at any fair offer.

Not readily knowing the answers to interviewers' questions.

This is why I spend the entire next chapter on common questions that interviewers ask. These are based on hundreds of debriefs I have performed over the years. Now, We do not have the answers to every possible question.

Win The Job - Interviewing for Success

It is incumbent upon you to **anticipate** and **rehearse** answers to tough questions about your background, such as a recent termination or an employment gap. Practicing with your spouse or a friend before the interview will help you to frame intelligent responses.

Remember, I offer specific, job winning verbiages in Chapters 3 and 5. Review these and make them your own, and you will have great success in getting the job you want.

This is another reason to find a good recruiter. At gpac, we represent over 100 industries and probably can help you find a great job. More than that, we will help you prepare for interviews and frame answers to those tough questions. For our candidates, our service is 100% free.

You can contact me at john.chisham@gogpac.com and I can direct you to someone that will be able to help you in your particular profession.

Relying too much on resumes.

This is close to not readily knowing the answers to the interviewers questions. They do not want to hear and answer like-just look on my resume! The truth is, employers hire people, not paper. Although a resume can list qualifications and skills, it's the **interview dialogue** that will portray you as a committed, responsive team player.

This is why it is important to know your resume. It must be an accurate portrayal of your true skillset. You make claims on your resume that must be backed up with actual numbers and statistics.

Win The Job - Interviewing for Success

Not asking for the job

This is one that perplexing. Why else would you interview if you did not want the job?

I have done follow up interviews with candidates and client companies, and have discovered many times that the one interviewing for the job acted as though they were uninterested and communicated that they had many other opportunities out there that may be more interesting.

I have also had to tell candidates that the reason no offer was coming was because of this tactic. They seemed to think it would light a fire underneath the company to come with an offer more quickly.

If you want the job, let the interviewers know. Make it very clear. More on this in the next chapter.

Remember, this is a business meeting, and you are giving a presentation of a product- you. Give a great presentation and prove your point and do not give the employer any reason to doubt what you are saying. At the end of the day, if you make a compelling argument and show that you are the only person for the job, you will get hired. I believe in you!

In the next chapter, It is my goal to help you prepare to answer and ask good questions in the interview. Review them and make them your own. They will help you win that job.

Chapter 5.
THE INTERVIEW:
INTERVIEWING TO WIN

The time has come. The interview itself is about to take place. You are ready.

A typical sequence of events for the interview are:

- Interview with personnel or HR (general questions, review of the company and their benefits.)
- Interview with the immediate supervisor and peers.
- Interview with the hiring authority (manager, etc.).

Sometimes this happens all at once, sometimes you are just doing one. However the interview is run, it is important to remember in order to win (get an offer) you must be fully engaged.

Win The Job - Interviewing for Success

- **Shake hands** (or whatever is offered- fist bump, elbow bump... if handshake, do so firmly
- **Sit down in the chair offered.** If none offered, ask, where should I sit?
- **Maintain eye contact** with the interviewer. If multiple interviewers, move your eyes through the room.
- **Maintain a high energy level.**
- **Sit up with back straight**.
- **Lean into the conversation**.
- **Pay attention** to tonality and speed of the person talking. Do your best to match speed and tone.
- **DO NOT imitate accents**.
- **Be yourself.** Poise, confidence, and self-respect are of great importance.

Through the entire process, conduct yourself with confidence and determination to get the job. You have other options, of course, and your interviewer knows this, but wants to think that you want a job with this company. **Sell yourself.** But do not come off desperate.

Open the interview and close the interview as though you want the job. Think about a blind date, or even a first date you have had. At the end of the date, both parties have some doubt as to whether the other party has interest- that is unless interest has been expressed verbally.

This is key - and it is what I call the "Blind Date Rule": Enter the interview expressing interest, and leave NO DOUBT as to your interest in the company, the position, and the interview.

Win The Job - Interviewing for Success

A sample was given in the last chapter:

"Mr/Ms/Mrs.____ Thanks for this opportunity to interview with your company. I have done some research, and I am excited to learn more about your company and about where it has been and where it is going"

Or else this is another version:
"Mr/Ms/Mrs.____, THANK YOU for scheduling time out of your busy day to interview me. I have done a lot of research about (company name) and have read and heard many positive things. I am excited to learn even more about the company and where I could possibly fit!

What this does is sets you up for a great interview that is more about a business conversation than it is an interrogation. It takes the pressure off of you and them and makes it more of a conversation.

And, a pro tip...use the same form of this prior to answering the money question....and at the conclusion of the interview. More on this later.

Interview Questions

The interview should be a **two-way conversation**. Ask questions of the interviewers. This shows your interest in the company and the position, and enables you to gather the right information to make an intelligent decision afterwards. The questions you have prepared can be asked to the different people you see.

Remember, the objective of the interview is to obtain an offer. During the interview, you must gather enough information concerning the position to make a decision.

Win The Job - Interviewing for Success

You should give complete but brief and relaxed answers to questions. Remember, there are two types of questions - the "what time is it" question and the "build me a clock" questions. For each type of question, you want to be concise and precise as possible. You should use questions that are asked of you as a basis for developing information that you want to make sure is presented. Remember, you are selling yourself with the goal of getting an offer.

When you are speaking about your previous jobs, do so in terms of duties and give indicators of good performance such as raises, sales volume, and promotions. Include short stories involving problems or challenges and how you were able to solve or overcome them. Results and numbers are called sizzle, and they will do you a great service in getting a job.

Answer a question to the best of your ability and then relax. If there is a period of silence before the interviewer asks the next question, stay calm. Interviewers often use silence to see if you can handle stress and maintain poise.

The following are types of questions you will likely be asked in an interview. Use the answers I provide as a guide. Do not memorize them as a script, but feel comfortable with the answers you will give. Make the answers your own. Add your personality and feel comfortable with your answers.

INTERVIEWER'S QUESTIONS

Exploring your Background Questions

Tell me about yourself.

Win The Job - Interviewing for Success

"Tell-me-about-yourself" means, "Tell me about your qualifications." Remember, this is an interview. Prepare a one to two- minute discussion of your qualifications- an elevator speech of sorts.

Start with education and discuss your experiences. Describe your performance (in raises, promotions, innovative designs, sales volume, increased profits, etc.) Answer these questions in terms of the qualifications required of the position. Keep responses **concise** and brief and avoid being derogatory or negative about previous jobs and bosses.

What are your greatest strengths?

Interviewers like to hear abstract qualities, expressed in concrete terms...

Loyalty, willingness to work hard, eagerness, fast-learner, technical skills, politeness, and promptness, are good examples Avoid simple generalizations like "*I like people.*" They are not helpful.

What are your greatest weaknesses?

Do not be intimidated. The interviewer probably wants reassurance that hiring you will not be a mistake. This is not the time to confess **all** of your imperfections. (Do not state "not being able to go to work on Mondays", or "coming in late", etc.).

Present your weaknesses as professional strengths, (i.e., "Sometimes work too hard to make sure things are done accurately" or "laser focussed on the task at hand."

Win The Job - Interviewing for Success

Be prepared to answer "How do you handle weaknesses?" because the answer to that question is far more important than the fact that you have weaknesses.

What do you do in your spare time?

Workaholics are not always the best employees. Present yourself as a well-rounded person. Your answer gives you dimension. Name some hobbies - but do not get too carried away on them. Your interviewer may have a limited time and if you get carried away on your hobbies and interests you may not learn all there is to know about the job.

Motive Questions

Answer motive questions enthusiastically. Show the interviewer that you are interested in the position and that you really want the job.

Remember to maintain eye contact and be sincere.

How can you contribute to this company?

Be positive and sell yourself. Make strong statements like

- "Bringing strong technical skills",
- "enthusiastic approach to problem solving"
- "desire to complete projects correctly and efficiently"

are some examples of concrete and strong responses.

Why should I hire you for this position?

Explain your qualifications and how you believe they are a "fit" the available position.

Win The Job - Interviewing for Success

Address your interest in the particular field and the specific job. Emphasize your ability to successfully perform the duties required. Also, note how the particular job is one you would have passion for and enjoyment performing.

Why do you want to work for our firm?

This is where your research comes in. Compliment what the company does, its location, its people, or its community involvement. Other positive remarks might be about the culture, the company's product or service, content of the position, or possibilities for growth or advancement.

Where do you hope to be in five years?

Having knowledge about conservative career progression in the field is vital- so be sure to have a good idea what can and cannot be achieved by the **ideal** candidate in the position.

Never tell the interviewer that "in five years, I want YOUR job" or something to the effect you feel you will be more successful than they are. You want to show a strong desire for career growth and advancement. Have confidence- but draw the line at calloused arrogance.

What interests you most about this position?

Here again, you have a chance to take advantage of your research and demonstrate your knowledge of the company.

Win The Job - Interviewing for Success

Do not tease the interviewer with a truthful one or two-word answer such as, "the challenge" or "the opportunity", This will force them to ask you to explain.

Instead of that, be very specific to the industry. If it is a sales job, for example, tell them "I love the challenge of killing what I eat- if I don't do the job I go hungry! It is also an opportunity to make uncapped income. I love to paid for my efforts! "

How long do you plan to be with this company?

Of course, employers want folks that will stay around. It is equally important that they do not sense you just want to collect a paycheck. A good answer might be "As long as I continue to learn and grow and am challenged to be a better version of myself".

What are your career goals?

Your answer should depend on a specific time frame:

Short term – "I want to be the best in my current position, while learning additional responsibilities. This, in itself, will assure my commitment to the firm and raise me to the next level of responsibility and promotion. I see myself wanting to stay technical but learn the necessary skills to lead people and projects."

Long term – "After proving my abilities, I see myself in a firm with the possibility of moving into a level of management that allows me to keep my skills sharp."

What are you doing to achieve your goals?

Win The Job - Interviewing for Success

"I look at continued learning as the key to success. I continue my education, as you see from my resume, by taking company educational courses, when offered, and college courses. I also read trade publications and magazines to keep me informed about the current and future directions in my field. When possible, I participate in professional organizations in my field."

Job Satisfaction Questions

Why did you leave your previous employer? OR Why do you want to leave your present employer?

NEVER speak poorly about a former employer. Be pleasant, be positive and be honest.

Your answer will probably be checked. Mention your desire to work for a more progressive company that offers more growth opportunities and recognition.

What did you like *most* about your previous job? What did you like *least* about your previous job?

An employer can evaluate the type of worker you will be by the items you choose. Cite specifics. You are also providing clues about the environment you seek. What you liked most can include a strong teamwork atmosphere, high- level of creativity, attainable deadlines. What you liked least should include any situations that you are unlikely to encounter in your new position.

Why are you looking for another job?

Again, be positive. I have to say that I have really enjoyed my years at ABC Construction. There are a lot of good people over there. But I am looking for a more progressive organization with greater opportunities for growth and recognition. I am looking for a team to join where I can make real contributions and advance my career.

What do you think your employer's obligations are to you?

Interviewers listen for employees who want a positive, enthusiastic, company atmosphere with the opportunity to advance. Such a person, they surmise, has motivation and staying power.

Are you applying for any other jobs?

In your answer, show that your search is geared for similar positions. This demonstrates a well-defined, focused objective. Make it known that your talents are applicable to other businesses and that you have explored ways to maximize your potential and are serious about finding the perfect opportunity. Do not give an indication that you are just shopping!

Performance Questions

What kind of decisions are most difficult for you?

Again, be truthful and admit not everything comes easily. Be careful what you do admit so as not to instantly disqualify yourself. Explain that you try to gather as much information and advice as you can to make the best decision possible.

Win The Job - Interviewing for Success

What are your greatest accomplishments?

Be honest, do not brag. This is a good time to point to specific career or educational highlights you have on your resume.

What causes you to lose your temper?

Everybody has a low boiling point on some particular issue. Pick one of yours; something safe and reasonable. People who are late to meetings, blame shifting, broken appointments and office "back-stabbing" are suitable responses. Do not say that you never fly off the handle. You will not be believed.

How do you feel about a younger, male/female boss?

A question like this usually means that your boss will either be younger or of the opposite gender or both. Be certain that if you register any concern, you will probably not be hired. Explain that their age or gender is of no importance to you. You are only interested in their capability and what you can learn from them.

What kind of worker are you?

Again, no one is perfect. Showing that you tackle every assignment with all of your energy and talents is admirable but mention that you also learn from your mistakes.

Salary Questions

What type of salary do you have in mind?

Win The Job - Interviewing for Success

Do not state a starting figure. A suitable reply:

Mr/Ms/Mrs _____, As I said earlier, I am very excited to learn about the company and the role I would be playing if hired. I have not been disappointed! So let us suffice it to say, I am looking for the right opportunity and I am confident that if you find that I am the best candidate for this position, you will extend me your best and most fair offer".

What is your current salary?

Answer truthfully. Remember that "salary" includes base, bonuses, commissions, benefits, and vacations as well as sick days and personal days. Also, if you are due a raise in the next three months, state the approximate percentage you expect.

Other questions you should be prepared to answer truthfully:

Are you willing to relocate?
May we check your references?
May we verify your income?

"I AM LOOKING FOR THE RIGHT OPPORTUNITY AND I AM CONFIDENT THAT IF YOU FIND THAT I AM THE BEST CANDIDATE FOR THIS POSITION, YOU WILL EXTEND ME YOUR BEST AND MOST FAIR OFFER."

Win The Job - Interviewing for Success

QUESTIONS FOR YOU TO ASK

Interviews should be a **two-way conversation**. If you want to have a successful interview, you must ask questions and take an active role in the interview. This demonstrates to the person interviewing you the importance you place on your work and career.

There are many benefits to asking questions. These include:

- Asking questions gives you a chance to demonstrate your depth of knowledge in the field
- Asking questions establishes an easy flow of conversation and relaxed atmosphere between you and the interviewer.
- Asking questions builds rapport

- Asking questions can help you determine if this job is right for you.
- Asking questions clarifies research you have done on the company in preparing for the interview.

Guidelines for good interview questions:

- Do not cross-examine the employer.
- Ask "open ended" questions requiring an explanation. Questions which can be answered with a "yes" or "no" are conversation stoppers.
- Do not interrupt when the employer is answering YOUR question.
- Ask job-relevant questions. Focus on the job –
 the company, products, services, people.
- **NEVER ask about money, benefits, vacation, etc**

Interest Questions

Prior to the interview, write your list of "Interest Questions" and take them with you.

- Ask about your potential peers, subordinates, and superiors.
- Take notes.
- Ask the employer how he/she got where they are today.

Why do you want someone for this job?

Ask the interviewer to explain why this job cannot be done by one of his current employees. The answer may give you a valuable job description.

Job Satisfaction Questions

Ask questions that relate to the responsibilities, importance, and authority of the position as well as

those investigating the rewards for a job well done and the long-range career opportunities.

What type of growth and advancement opportunities does this position and the company offer?

This tells the interviewer that you have a long-term vision for your professional future and that you're not just looking for a paycheck; you're looking to secure a career.

How do you see me benefiting the company?

Finding out why you were selected out of possibly hundreds of other candidates gives you a chance to expand on the qualities that caught their eye, further making the case for your hire.

What would my first project be if I'm hired? This will give you a specific idea of what you can expect when you walk into the office that first day after hired. It also can give you a heads up as to what will be expected of you, allowing you to build on those attributes during the interview.

Are continuing education and professional training stressed? This shows your willingness to learn new skills and adapt to new challenges or initiatives. Adaptability is important in today's fickle economy and could be key to retaining your job in a reorganization.

Why did you choose this company? Hearing why a current employee opted to work at the firm can give you some insight into some of the strengths and opportunities within the organization.

What is the company's culture?

This will reveal those "intangibles" of a company that have nothing to do with professional experience or education. If you need a traditional, office/cube environment to stay focused and get the job done, more creativity-driven workplace which allows music streaming from computers, hoop tournaments and ultra-flexible schedules may not be conducive to your productivity.

Win The Job - Interviewing for Success

Who will evaluate me if I'm hired?
Ask this question, and you'll discern the company and departmental structure under which you will be. For instance, will you report directly to the vice president or will there be a succession of middle managers between you?

Performance Questions

Why is this position not being filled from within the company?

You may discover that nobody in this organization would accept it or that your future fellow employees are a weak lot.

How many people have held this job in the last five years? Were they promoted or did they leave the company?

If the turnover has been high, you have a right to suspect that the job may leave something to be desired. Or it could mean that you can expect to be promoted quickly.

What exactly are the job responsibilities?"

Job ads usually list the general areas of responsibility for a position. It's always good to confirm what the actual duties will be. You don't want to start your new job as an engineer and find out you're responsible for the weekly doughnut run.

How did you get started in the company?

A good way to get to know the interviewer better and gain insight into the promotional path the company follows.

Win The Job - Interviewing for Success

What are examples of the best results produced by people in this job?

Here you may discover you are overqualified or in a position to ask for considerably more money.

When will a decision be made on the successful candidate?"

Knowing this helps you determine the timing of your interview follow-up activities.

May I contact you if I have other questions?

It's always good to wrap up the interview with this question. It keeps the door open for further, giving you one last chance to make your case.

Additional Questions:

- What would my responsibilities and duties be?
- What are the most difficult aspects of the position?
- Describe a typical day on the job.
- Describe the department's/company's growth in the next two years.
- What is the philosophy on training and development here?
- Has there been downsizing within the company? How is it handled?
- How do you think I would fit into the job and into your organization?
- What projects would I be involved in now? In the future?
- Who would I be working for and with?
- What is the person doing who used to hold this position?
- When would you need me to start?
- May I see my work area?
- May I meet some of my future co-workers?

Interview Conclusion

If you are sincerely interested in the position and are satisfied with the answers given, you should ask the interviewer if he/she feels that you are qualified for the position. This gives you another chance to review points that may need clarification. Illustrate confidence in your abilities and convince the interviewer that you are capable of handling the position successfully.

Ask for the job.

Do not play coy. Think about the blind date, or even a first date you have had. At the end of the date, both parties have some doubt as to whether the other party has interest, unless of course there is verbal communication setting expectations as well as a possible second date.

So, **If you want the job, ask for it.** Do not play around and act as though it is not important to you, or that you have many other options - even if you do.

Make a positive statement about the position. Emphasize that this is exactly the type of opportunity you have been looking for and would like to be offered the position.

Ask when you should expect an answer. A typical conclusion might be:

"Mr/Ms/Mrs.____, THANK YOU again for scheduling time out of your busy day to interview me. I have certainly learned a lot today, and I like what I have learned. I would like to join your team.

Win The Job - Interviewing for Success

I know I would be an asset to you/your department because you need someone who can , and . As you know, I have (match your qualifications the employer's "hot buttons").

Before I leave, do you have any more questions about my background or qualifications or can I supply you with any more information? On a scale of 1 to 5, how do I compare to the other candidates you have interviewed?

I can start as soon as **you need me.** *(Or after appropriate notice to your current employer)*

At this point there should be no doubt in the interviewers' mind as to whether you want the job or not. The farewell should include a smile, direct eye contact, a firm but gentle handshake (or fist bump).

How am I to follow up?

We will go into great detail in the next chapter about what to do in the hours and days following the interview. Before you leave the building, make sure you ask about the timeline. That is, you need to know who is making the final hiring decision and by when they will make it.

You should also be proactive and ask about your own follow up. You should ask "When will you make a decision about this position? May I call you to follow up after (determined date/time)?

This brings up a very important factor. Make sure you have the appropriate contact information to follow up, This should include names, phone numbers, and e-mail addresses of everyone in on the interview process.

Win The Job - Interviewing for Success

Walk out of the building and get into your mode of transportation. You are done. Go to the next chapter and get the next steps to follow after the interview. You are not done yet! There are still steps to take to get all you can out of the interview process and to guarantee a very good shot at winning that job!

Chapter 6
AFTER THE INTERVIEW:
THE WAITING GAME

You have done all you can do in terms of the interview-
now is the waiting game.
But you certainly do not want to waste your time waiting.
In fact, there are several things you can be doing in the
hours and days as you sit and wait
for the decision.

This time should be very productive. Until you have an
offer to consider, all you can do is continue what you
are doing.

What should you do in the minutes, hours, and
days following the interview?

Win The Job - Interviewing for Success

Deconstruct the interview

If you have time, you should go find a place away from the interview location to sit and review what just happened. Take out your notebook and notes and review in

your mind what happened in the interview. Try to review every detail of the interview. Try to remember what you did well. Also review where you felt you fell short, maybe an answer to a question you should clarify.

This is also an important time to review how the interviewer answered your questions.

- Did you get all your questions answered?

- What were your impressions of the office atmosphere?
- Can you see yourself spending a lot of time there, or is this just going to be a coffee break?

This is important- because you are determining how hard you want to go after this job, or if it will not be a fit.

- Is this company someplace you can see fitting into and growing long term?
- does the company align with your career goals?

Write all these things down while they are fresh in your mind. You will want to review them in the days to come- and use them in your follow up correspondence.

Write a Thank You Letter

Make sure that within 24 hours following the interview that you send an e-mail expressing thanks. If you have followed the advice I have given you, you already know the verbiage. It is basically the same as you have been repeating throughout the interview:

Win The Job - Interviewing for Success

"Mr/Ms/Mrs.____, THANK YOU again for scheduling time out of your busy day to interview me. I certainly learned a lot today, and I like what I have learned.

Obviously, if there were multiple people in the interview, it adds a very good touch to use the same format, but personalize it for each individual person. There is a very good chance that the team will share your thank you- so no two e-mails should be exactly the same.

Insert a couple of highlights about how you believe you will fit in, and how you can bring value to the business and to the team you will work with.

Finish the letter like this *"I look forward to hearing from you by (insert date discussed). If you have any other questions that will help you in your decision process, please do not hesitate to call".*

Writing a thank-you letter is a **very important step,** whether you want the job or not. If you discover you do not want the job, the letter obviously is a little different. You still thank the interviewer for their time. You conclude the letter by sharing with them that you have determined that this job would not be the right fit for you, and give them a reason. This will keep doors open for the future should you change your mind.

For the most part, an e-mail will do the job. However, you might consider the type of place that you are applying. If it is more of an old-school and traditional place of work, you might consider an e-mail **and** a traditional snail mail. This approach has a couple of benefits, not the least of which is keeping you top of mind with the hiring authorities.

Send a LinkedIn connection request

Win The Job - Interviewing for Success

If you have done what I advised in chapter 4, and cleaned up your social media, this would be a great time to send a connection request to the people who interviewed you and follow the company as well.

Like the thank-you note, it should be individually tailored. You only have 300 characters in a LinkedIn connection notice so it should go something like this:

"It was great meeting you at ABC Company and hearing about your experiences and the XYZ position.

I am very interested in the position and joining your team. In the meantime, I would like to add you to my LinkedIn network"

Best, [Your name]

When the connection is made, do not take advantage of the connection and spam the person who interviewed you or harass them about the decision to hire you. Stick to the time schedule everyone agreed to as far as follow up.

Complete any "Homework" The company gives you

Win The Job - Interviewing for Success

There are many tasks that you may be asked to complete if the company is interested. Some of these are handled prior to the interview, but some might be asked for in a follow up. It is important that you complete these tasks in a competent as well as timely manner.

A few of these include:

- Psychological tests like DISC or the Predictive Index
- Job specific tests to check skill level
- Background check paperwork

Doing these in a thoughtful and timely manner communicate interest to the company. Doing

them in a thoughtful manner shows good work ethic and may lead to a higher offer if you show great aptitude!

Follow up

When walking out of the interview, you should have asked the interviewers when and with whom to follow up. If you did forget to do that, a good rule of thumb is to follow up one week after you send a thank you note. Follow up with the decision maker, whether it be with HR or the hiring manager.

There is a fine line between expressing desire to get to work with a team and sounding desperate and confrontational. The former is what you want to do, so make sure to ask when you can follow up with the hiring manager again if they do not yet have an answer.

Other questions you might ask to gauge the interest of the company:
- Where are you at in the hiring process?
- How many people have interviewed? How many more need to interview?
- How do I compare to the other candidates that have interviewed?
- Are there any questions that need to be clarified from my interview that would help you make a decision in my favor?
- Is there any reason you would not hire me vs. any of the candidates you have interviewed?
- When do you foresee making a final decision?

"THERE IS A FINE LINE BETWEEN EXPRESSING DESIRE TO GET TO WORK WITH A TEAM AND SOUNDING DESPERATE AND CONFRONTATIONAL".

Keep Up the Job Search

If you have a job, continue doing your job well. If you have other interviews, take the time to prepare. Continue the process. Do not take yourself off the market. The goal is to get the job that you want; but you do not know all the information if you sit and wait between interviews. Keep up the process. The busier you are with interviewing, the less time you have to worry about the answer coming. Until you have an offer in your hand, your job is to find the best fit for you.

The Conclusion: Offer or Rejection

The goal of the process that you have just concluded is to get the job.

I believe if you have the skillset to do the actual job, and you learn the skillset of interviewing with the skills in this book, you give yourself an excellent chance to win the job that you want.

At the end of the day, however, you will either receive an offer to come work for the company or a rejection. If you have been engaged in the follow up process, you will likely know what the answer is before it comes. What I mean is, if you ask the right questions and listen to the answers you will have a great idea what the outcome will be.

You got an offer- now what?

As many companies as there are, there are many different ways to present an offer. Some companies will start with some kind of verbal offer. If you receive a verbal offer, the best bet is to thank the person giving the offer, and let them know that you would like to see the offer in writing.

It can a response like this:

"Thank you so much for the offer- I am excited for the opportunity. Will you be sending a written offer? When you do, when do you need a response by?"

In doing so, you are communicating excitement, desire to work for the company, but also that you will need a written offer to review before acceptance. This gives you time to make a well-informed decision.

For our purposes, for the rest of this chapter we will go on the assumption that you are already dealing with some form of a written offer. Written offers can be as simple as a one page offer to a multiple page formal contract detailing everything about the job description, hours of work, vacation time, benefits, and etc. Whatever form it comes in, there is a few things you must do.

Acknowledge receipt

If the offer is written, the first thing you must do is to acknowledge that you received it.

I recommend sending an acknowledgement directly to the e-mail from which you received it. If it is from a person other than who interviewed you, you may want to also add them as a CC. In your acknowledgement e-mail, you will want to thank the company for the offer. Then, promise to review it. Finally, you want to ask for a date and time they will need your final decision.

Review the offer

Depending on the type of job you are applying for, an offer of employment can be very simple and or very complex. I have seen simple one page offer letters detailing salary, benefits, other compensation, and start date. Other offer letters have been multiple pages long in very small print.

Win The Job - Interviewing for Success

Your best bet is to sit down with someone else to get a second set of eyes on the offer. If you are using a recruiter (as I recommend) that recruiter can be a very valuable resource- and can be a very good second set of eyes. This is less about reviewing legal mumbo jumbo and more about making sure the offer is what you are looking for in terms of compensation, perks, benefits, etc.

Take the time to do research on standard rates of pay for the job responsibilities n the area you are working. If the money and other perks are right, and in line with the area, you simply need to decide if the culture, location, and other subjective areas make this the right fit for you.

If needed, prepare a counter-offer

Many times the money, hours, and position have been so clearly communicated prior to the offer stage that there is no need. I always encourage companies to come with their best offer. However, this is not always the case. If the offer is below what you expected after factoring in all of the other company benefits, you might want to negotiate a more fitting salary.

Begin your e-mail with a statement of interest and enthusiasm for the job. It does not hurt to thank the company again for considering you! Remember to include your key- selling points such as how you plan to contribute to the company and what you believe you bring to the table. Remember, a company looks at bringing someone on that will save them money off the bottom line, or make them money on the top. Emphasize the added value you bring and what really sets you apart.

Now write your counter offer. This should be a salary That is supported by your research on the market and what you bring to the company. This also should be supported by current market realities. Again, having a recruiter on your team will help you determine what your current value is. If you do not have access to a recruiter, you can gauge real interest by the number of interviews and the urgency of the company to get you on board. Bottom line: if you like the company and the culture and they are paying you better than you are being paid now, it should be an easy choice.

Be ready for the company to come back either way, rejecting or accepting your counteroffer. Whatever the

outcome, show your gratitude, and leave the conversation on a high note. Never burn a bridge.

Accept or Reject the Offer

Now that you have reviewed the offer, and have come to your decision, you need to let the company know. Whether you accept or reject, the method is the same. You are going to send an e-mail that formally lets the company know of the decision. It is important in this e-mail to communicate gratitude to those who have been in this process with you, especially if you are turning down the offer.

Here is a sample acceptance e-mail:

I wanted to formally thank you for the job offer at [Company Name]. I am excited to begin working with you on [start date}, learning more about the company and finding the best ways to contribute my skills to the team.

Please reach out at any time if you need anything else from me prior to the start date. The best way to contact me is through [email], but feel free to call me as well at [number].

Again, thank you for this opportunity. I can't wait to begin working for such a talented team.

Sincerely, [Your Name]

And if you are rejecting the offer:

I wanted to formally thank you for the job offer at [Company Name]. I genuinely enjoyed meeting your team and learning about your company.

However, I have decided to go another direction with my next career stop. I am grateful to have found another company that offers a position that is more aligned with my current career goals.

Again, thank you for this opportunity. I wish the best for everyone I have met at [company name]. I hope we can work together at some point in the future.

Sincerely, [Your Name]

Turn in your notice

Once you have a signed offer letter and a start date you need to turn in your notice to your current employer. Many people I talk to are afraid of this step, but it is very important. The standard notice is two weeks; depending on your industry and responsibility, this can vary. Some companies will let you go immediately, while others will ask you to finish projects and this date will push out one month. Regardless of the time, as soon as you accept the job, you need to turn in your notice.

There are differing ways to do this- face to face or by writing an e-mail. This depends on the relationship you have with the manager. My recommendation is hybrid; I believe you should bring a letter and meet with the manager face to face.

This is a simple process, no need to overcomplicate it. Similar to all the other interactions we have spoken about, do it with respect and gratitude. The letter is formal, short to the point.

Dear [manager name, company address] ,

I have decided to move on from [company name] and this is my formal two week's notice.I

n my [tenure] at [company name] I have learned many things about [type of business] which has made me a better [job role or function]. For my personal and professional development in this time at the company, I will forever be grateful.

However, I have found a position at a new company that will (improve my career trajectory OR challenge me OR provide growth in this area OR increase my responsibility)

I will wrap up any duties that need to be performed with the same care and professionalism I have displayed in my tenure her.

Thank You, [your name]

Depending on your relationship with the manager, the notice can go quickly. In most cases there will be questions. Just like in the interview process, be prepared to answer the questions with honesty, respect, and gratitude. You do not want to burn bridges.

There are questions you can answer, and there are others you should refrain from answering specifically:

-What company are you going to work for?

-How much are they paying you? (any question about compensation is not appropriate)

-Any question that makes you feel uncomfortable

Any question that forces you to speak ill of a person or process

A word about counter offers:

If you are any good at your job, or if there is a high demand for the type of job you are in you will likely get a counteroffer. You must remember- you started this interview process for a reason. Now that you have landed a new position that means more money, a better situation, and new opportunities, **you must remember why you began looking in the first place!**

Win The Job - Interviewing for Success

Imagine: when you give notice to your current employer, your boss says, "Tell me what they offered. I'll match it or beat it." Now what do you do? Before jumping at a counteroffer, think long and hard. Ask yourself this – If you were worth X dollars yesterday, why is your company suddenly willing to now pay you Y dollars today? Accepting a counteroffer can have numerous negative consequences - not the least of which is burning a bridge at the place you just accepted a great position.

Consider these top 10 reasons to say "no" to a counteroffer:

1: What type of company do you work for if you have threatened to resign before they give you what you're worth?

2: Where is the money for the counteroffer coming from? Is it your next raise, early? (Many companies have strict wage and salary guidelines that must be followed).

3: Your company will immediately start looking for a new person at a lower salary. They are likely buying time by extending you an counter-offer

4: You have now made your employer aware that you are unhappy. From this day on, your loyalty will always be in question.

5: When promotion time comes around, your employer will remember who was loyal and who wasn't. Which list do you think you will be on?

6: When times get tough, your employer will begin the cutback with you.

7: The same circumstances that now cause you to consider a change will repeat themselves in the future, even if you accept a counteroffer.

8: Statistics compiled by the National Employment Association confirm the fact that over 80% of those people who elected to accept a counteroffer are not with their company six months later.

9: Accepting a counteroffer is a bribe and a blow to your personal pride. Were you bought?

10: Once the word gets out, the relationship that you now enjoy with your co-workers will never be the same. You will lose the personal satisfaction of peer group acceptance.

You need to think carefully about all these facts before making a final decision. Evaluate your reasons for leaving your current position, the reasons you accepted the position, and what your career goals are. A mistake in your career could cost you your future, professional growth and money. Usually when it comes down to it, you're better off saying "no" to a counteroffer.

Last words: You have done it!

Congratulations. Now our journey has come to an end!

You have gotten the job, and you have done so in a professional manner. You should be very proud of yourself.

Win The Job - Interviewing for Success

As you begin this new chapter in your career, make sure your first hours, days, and weeks are spent diving in, being engaged, learning and listening about the ways in which you can bring value to your new company. Enjoy the new journey and embrace the new challenge.

ABOUT THE AUTHOR

John B. Chisham is a professional headhunter for gpac. He has prepared thousands of people for interviews and has a very high success rate, proven out over time with multi-million dollars in placement fees. He has spent 4 consecutive years as the #1 recruiter in his industry.

John lives in Sioux Falls, SD with his wife Cindy. He spends his spare time cooking - (grill master) , golfing, traveling, and chasing grandkids.

If you like this book, please leave a review at oneeightycoach.com and tell the world the story of your successful job hunt!

If you are a seeking a specific position, and could use the help of a **recruiter**, please reach out to me at john.chisham@gogpac.com

If you are interested in coaching services, I take on a limited amount of clients each month. If you are interested, please reach out to me at john@oneeightycoach.com

My coaching specialties include:
Life Coaching
Business Coaching
Ministry Coaching
Leadership Development
Financial Coaching

www.ingramcontent.com/pod-product-compliance
Lightning Source LLC
Chambersburg PA
CBHW081626220526
45467CB00029B/3131